Before the Last Petal Falls

poetry & prose

BY:

MLIVV | *Jessica Livia*

ISBN: 978-1-962072-06-9

Cover art & design by: Melissa M. Combs

**Octave
Eight**
PUBLISHING
∞

octaveeightpublishing@gmail.com

Before the Last Petal Falls

poetry & prose

BY:

MLIVV | *Jessica Livia*

"And I pray one prayer —I repeat it til' my tongue
stiffens — Catherine Earnshaw, may you not rest as
long as I am living; you said I killed you —
haunt me, then!"

-Heathcliff, WUTHERING HEIGHTS

Dedicated to *Matina Livia*, my daughter. You inspire me to do things I never thought possible. I pray in life you chase your passions to the fullest, never give up or settle for anything less than extraordinary. I pray you love passionately. And though there will be heartbreak in life, I pray you never let it discourage you, and you learn and grow from it. I hope you know love is the most important thing in the world and love exists in *all realms*; you never lose it, it just transforms. Your heart is so kind and pure. I'm so proud of you and all we are accomplishing everyday together.

I love you to infinity in this life and the next.

LOVE ALWAYS, *Mommy.*

I've been imprisoned by your lies,
stuck in the hopes of what could be,
and lying to myself about what truly is.
I await my fate and

the injustice
      LOVING you
          has caused.

I feel the doom in the air
as I await the night of my heart's
execution and what my final words will be.
I hope now you see what your betrayal
has caused me —
my life, and all the years I can't replace.

But even with a final breath,
and a goodbye
to that girl you shattered down slowly,
I mutter with my last glance at you,

I'll LOVE you always.

I cry in rhymes now,
as if my sorrow creates lullabies;
my HEART'S song.

Everyone is so used to my tears,
it's becoming music to their ears.

I'm not sure where, along the lines,
my pain transformed into
that catchy song, stuck in everyone's head.

My pain became a number one best-seller.
But I'm happy my dread
somehow turned into the rhymes.
They hum of PAIN
they secretly leave unsaid.

A skeleton of who I was,
engulfed in this sweet decay, accepting dismay
for what we have is far to beautiful to betray.

You have my heart as we dance under moonlit skies.
As stars ★ GLIMMER ★,
I see my broken beauty in your eyes.

And though we finally found true love, everything
perfect is destined to die. So embrace me as I am;
as I seek solace in your soul.

Our petals wilted,
yet the colors remain.
Ethereal beauty preserved
with time.
Our LOVE still thrives,
and our MADNESS survives,
as we love through endless nights
of moonlight,
and dance to nature's orchestra,
while time slips away.
LOVE and your SMILE
a r e all that remain.

You spun me in a web of emotions,
and left me in your
HAUNTED HEART.
I've never been more intertwined
in something so dangerous.

You hurt me and left me
hanging on,
yet still
I'm tangled in these feelings
I can't break free from.
Nor do I think I want to.
I think I'm bound too tightly
to these emotions,
to let go.

At least you wrapped me tight enough
to keep me warm, I suppose.

Our legs tangled in bed sheets,
watching **HORROR MOVIES.**
Endless nights
surrounded by candles,
as the leaves swirled in the cool air
that seeped through my window.

What I thought turned into love
died with the last candle's flame.

It started with **HORROR MOVIES,**
then ended with nightmares
of you alone in bed, holding onto

my **SEPTEMBER SINS.**

Nothing HAUNTS us more
than the unspoken words
we refuse to say.
As time passes
and the chance is taken
away, we are left in regret,
yearning to be back in
the moment where
we can just mutter those few words
that may have altered our mournful fate.

Maybe if I said
I LOVE YOU
just a few more times,
I wouldn't be sitting here
wondering if you knew.
Times when I'm silent,
my tears are unlocked,
so these unsaid words
become a flowing of regret
that I dread.

I let this flesh I'm in
become a HAUNTED HOUSE,
forever frozen in our favorite season,
holding our sins hostage,
laying you to rest in my soul,
as your spirit roams these bones I carry
so heavily.

I'll make this HAUNTED HEART a place
THE GHOST of our love can feel at home.

I inhaled your laced lies
and drew my last breath of hope.
You were the one destined
to destroy my heart,
yet your intoxicating ways
forced me to stay.

Now bleeding INK,
to rue the memories
I keep imprisoned in my mind
away.

I crave your kiss,
because your lips
left scars on my skin.
You were such a
　　　　PRETTY POISON
　　　　　　to digest.

I crave your kiss,
because your lips
left scars on my skin.
You were such a

pretty poison

to digest.

Together our flame burnt so bright
it attracted unwanted attention.

I wish it could just be the two of us
and the surrounding world
would fade away;
that I could rid my days of
these judgements for
LOVING YOU,
and live in a place free of misery,
mocking gestures,
and envious eyes.
A place I can just
LOVE YOU
like I'm meant to,
by letting the world slip away,
leaving just *you and I*.

Fall in love with the girl who's heart is a haunted house, filled with tales of love from other realms. She'll leave you in emotions you'll crave to understand, and feelings you never knew you had. She'll leave you intrigued by DARKNESS yet engulfed in a warmth she emits from passions so strong. She's the girl who loves FALL and BOOKS, and who craves deep conversation over coffee. When winter falls, she's the one your mind won't be able to escape. She's a blizzard of peculiar. She'll leave you begging for her oddness, and craving those nights in bed, wrapped in one another, watching horror movies. The two of you tangled in bed sheets, as she haunts your mind and possesses your body —- she's the girl you'll NEVER want to escape.

When we met,
we collided in a way
that merged our souls.
So though our relationship
didn't work, and its time to part,
you will carry a piece of me
in all you do,
and likewise,
I will carry you too.

It makes saying goodbye
a bit beautiful —
to know,
though we weren't meant for forever,
you were a BEAUTIFUL getaway.

When night comes,
lets shed the skin we're in,
fly above the ground,
and love without expectations.
Lets carry nothing but each other
through realms and laugh as we
soar through skies
never seen by human eyes.

Lets carry nothing but our souls,
as we admire moons so brilliantly constructed.

Lets HAUNT worlds,
then come back home,
hop into our bodies and get ready
for that perfect morning coffee,
with a kiss.

Your indecency
hung like a tapestry
of lies
on my wall.
The ornate designs
weaved in shades of red,
as to warn me
you were dangerous
and to stay away.
But I've always been
intrigued by
BEAUTIFULLY
misleading things.

The leaves are changing and so are your feelings towards me. I can feel the change in you as I feel the change in the air. The weather is not the only thing turning cold. Your soul is getting ready to freeze over, faster than the first snowfall. And though your silence is deafening, as I absorb your loveless lies, I leave my heart with you. Maybe in the spring when we unfreeze and you see me next to you still, maybe then you'll **LOVE ME.**

I can't think of a better way to define poetic justice.
I'm trying to let this go and be happy, but my mind is
saying "FUCK THAT." I worshipped you once, now
you'll be just a memory that inspired me to rhyme.
You'll see ALL YOU HAD in time. I can only pray by
then I have someone who deserves me, because each
day that passes and you're not next to me, I only grow
stronger; more used to your absence. I'm fighting for
my happiness, every second; fighting to put all those
pieces of me you smashed in anger, back together,
so I can see my reflection once more.

Remember that poem
I wrote for you in the past.
I guess ETERNITY didn't last.

Let this pain not be in vain.
I can no longer be part of your reality,
so I will now invade your dreams
and curse your slumber
to where you cannot,
no matter what you do,
shut me out.

I will linger there all hours of the night
as a reminder of the pain you've caused me.
I will make sure my pain devours every corner
of your subconscious,
til' the GHOST of my memory
haunts your every sleepless night.

Our heartbreak was serendipitous.
Though I may no longer feel it,
I'm grateful I now get the chance
to one day be loved
COMPLETELY, EFFORTLESSLY
and DESPARATELY.
And although I'll always carry love in my heart for
you, you also deserve that life-altering love,
and the butterflies in your belly kinda feeling.
So even though we left it all to chance, and it didn't
last, I will always consider our heartbreak a stepping
stone to happiness for us both.

I'll cherish such an accidental
collision of TWO SOULS,
searching for our once in a lifetime.

I can't say I was never a thief,
because
I have stolen a part of your SOUL,
and I *cannot* give it back.

I actually can't live without it.
So is it stealing when it's something
my soul needs to survive?

I know I'll face punishment for my deeds,
yet what a misfortune it would be
not to carry even
the smallest piece of you within me.

Though stealing is bad,
the heavens would be sad
if we weren't in someway still together.
So forgive me,
but I love you too much to let go of
the piece I've taken.

I promise I'll take care of it ETERNALLY,
and if you shall ever falter,
the part of you I hold,
I will use to CARRY YOU through.

I know I'm still in denial.
I'm starting a new life without you,
and despite your deception,
I hope you find happiness too.

THE DEVIL was once the most beautiful angel,
and you wear YOUR WINGS much like his.

I now understand the gallantry of something that's
supposed to be so terrifying,
being so absolutely ANGELIC.

I was too blind to see your lies,
all because I saw those ANGEL EYES.
You wore such a handsome disguise.

It's hard to think I am going
to have to be loyal to someone else
one day,
but I will learn overtime,
and believe what
you once told me —
that nobody will ever be you and I.

I hope that's TRUE,
because I never want to be put through
what you put me through again.

I never want to hear those words.
You said, "I'm just glad
I was strong enough to finally say goodbye,
and I don't have to live a lie."

I heard them say,
"I think you went CRAZY."
But I was already mad
the moment I laid eyes on you.
My fate sealed.

Your hand was meant for me to hold.
It would be a beautiful story told —
not one with a happy ending, yet one
leaving everyone yearning for a love
they can go insane for.
A love that would make you do intangible things.
I'd dig us a grave just to know
you'd be next to me for ETERNITY.

I'd introduce myself to the vines and rocks
beneath the dirt,
for that's where we will share forever.
That'd be our home.
Maybe it's crazy,
and simple minds can't understand
something so beautifully irrational,
as you and me.

What if ghosts don't haunt us,
but we are actually haunting them
as daily reminders of what they left behind.
No more sleep to ESCAPE,
just ALWAYS AWAKE,
stuck in our realm,
unseen and unheard,
imprisoned here
by our sorrow that holds them here.
Yet they can't comfort us.

It's a NOTION that
gnaws at MY MIND.

I hope I'm wrong,
and our love is enough
to set them free…
not to ever be stuck here,
but *free* in the in-between.

You found beauty
in killing me SLOWLY.
No wonder your favorite season was fall.
I had to surrender to heartache.
I wasn't strong enough to fight back.
You must've smelled my vulnerability,
like a scavenger
and hunted me down.

I was desperate for LOVE.
I was your PERFECT PREY.

You must've smelled my
vulnerability
like a scavenger
and hunted me down.

I was *desperate for love.*
I was your

perfect prey.

My heart dropped as fast
as the first leaf,
as AUTUMN was awoken out of her sleep.
The first brisk wind blew,
tearing through my mind.

The start of fall —
things begin to die,
and so did our love,
just in time.

Our love,
now the ghost
that roams these streets,
looking for a new home,
watching the honey combs wither.
My soul shivers, our love,
now lost in this world
FULL OF DISMAY.

Now skeletons and bones,
I pray you never leave me alone.

Like a Raven circling its prey,
even at my DARKEST,
please stay.
Do not leave me in these
meadows alone.

Before dawn,
I hand you my vivacity, drawn.
I will hand you each ounce of me
in hopes you'll see
FOREVER is long,
and with you is where I belong.

Our hearts beat to the same rhyme,
always meant to be,
just never the right time.
As your shadow crosses mine,
it's no surprise our love is simply divine,
cradled by light.
Even if we fight it,
we simply fell in love
at an unfortunate time —
where even the TRUEST LOVE can be
lost, no matter the mournful cost.

If you should die before I do,
I do not wish you peace.
I pray you STAY WITH ME
until my final breath.
I wish you the same misery
that I will endure,
every single day,
with my every breath.
I will not be able to touch you.
So become MY GHOST,
and let me hear your moans.
Remind me constantly
that you're right here.
Because the pain I will feel without you
wouldn't truly be a life worth living,
but a mere existence.

So maybe this all sounds morbid,
but promise me, in this life, and the next,
you'll possess my soul in any and every realm —
PROMISE no matter the circumstances,
you'll NEVER LEAVE ME by myself.

Fall —

it haunts me as it returns each year,
reminding me
I know all to well
what it's like to die slowly,
and simultaneously
be alive.

It reminds me of the beauty everyone sees
while I am withering away,
a BEAUTIFUL FACE
can be as deceiving
as the allure of nature dying
to be reborn every year.

You leave me BROKEN and TORN,
but still all you will see
is the BEAUTY, not the PAIN.
Every year it's the same.

As the fields become
barren,
the emptiness brings
a sort of clarity.

My mind was cluttered
by the BEAUTY of your face.
And now that you're gone,
I see clearly
all the false affections
I foolishly chased.

I was nothing more than a flesh contraption
for your pleasure;
a weapon used against boredom.
Though I will never stand a chance
against a soul destroying succubus,
(your touch, INTOXICATING;
your words ALLURING.)

I never thought a little bit of ecstasy
would be a diversion from the sanity
I clung to.

You took your shot,
and in a mere moment of weakness
I submitted to you,
and engulfed your pain.
I absorbed it like
TAINTED SUNLIGHT.

Now rid me
of these false feelings,
and restore my essence.
It was never yours to toy with.

My faith will deflect the DARKNESS
in your HEATHEN HEART.

I submitted to you,
and engulfed your pain.
I absorbed it like

tainted sunlight.

Her eyes,
astonishingly BEAUTIFUL,
told such tragic stories.

They told of her former happy years,
then the one moment
that broke her spirit
and left those BEAUTIFUL eyes
in endless tears,
for the remainder of her years.

I have been consistently loyal to you
through all of your false-hearted phases.
Saying,
just like the moon,
you will change,
become whole,
and your devotion will shine upon
the darkest of waters,
leaving it glowing
for the Gods themselves to
marvel at something so
beautifully faithful.

But am I crazy,
still awaiting the day
you will fill the sky with your faults,
leaving them amongst the stars,
and you will come, true-hearted,
back to me FOREVER?
Or am I truly fantasizing a fairytale ending
out of mere passion?

I just want my
HAPPILY EVER AFTER.

I let each lie spill

crimson black,

dripping to my lips,
so you can taste the pain
you caused.
Your recipe.
You wrote each
ingredient
so perfectly,
then marked it —

her pain for **my pleasure.**

I devoured your SIN-KISSED lips.

Like poring honey
on my tongue,
your sweet nectar
tastes like dishonor.
Your silky smooth skin
feels sacrilegiously FLAWLESS.

It's as if the Gods themselves
are staring at me in judgement,
knowing your injustices
will reveal me in sorrow;
knowing I should be stronger.

But how can I be,
when you're my favorite taste
of FORBIDDEN SACCHARINITY?

There's nothing left of you.
The wind came and blew
every trace of you away.
Yet there's still a chill
I get in my body
of something missing.

I think it's my subconscious,
reminiscing
of a time,
of a warmth,
even THE SUN was jealous of.

I hear you banging on my door.
I'd open,
but I'm too comfortable
in my SELF-LOVE phase
to hear all of your bullshit lies.
Leave your dishonesty at the door.

It was a rollercoaster of emotions
that we were on.
You bought season passes,
so I burnt the amusement park
you made of our relationship
to the ground.

One match, and
I SET MYSELF FREE.

I whisper secrets
to the SUNFLOWERS,
then they turn their face
and whisper my secrets to
the SUN.
I feel as if each ray that hits
my skins is a cosmic cradle
of pure devotion
shining down,
saying,
"I know you've been hurt,
but KEEP GOING."

As the day begins
I stop to reminisce of yesterday's kiss,
and the way you touched me.
It was everything I thought it would be.
It was filled with consummate elegance.
But I soon learned even a night
of pure perfection
can end in rejection.
You only wanted me for a night,
while I craved you FOR A LIFETIME.
So as I peel away the skin of yesterday
and rid myself of every trace of you,
I will put it in the back of my memory
as the time I learned
I can't let JUST ANYBODY in.

Truthfully
you need to be little weird
to love my mind fully.
And in order to do that,
you need to understand
the shadows I carry.
I'm a bit of DARKNESS
dipped in GOLD —
the perfect mix
of twisted, yet serene.

The nights grow longer
by candlelight,
and the days shorter.

I'll savor you
every extra minute.
I'll revel in each inch of you,
as the leaves wrinkle,
and so does our skin.

If I could choose my
last moments, they'd be right here
WITH YOU.

I remember
being young and innocent
and hearing about
dishonor and lies,
and how men cheat,
thinking that's just something
you hear about.
I would think to myself,
it's rare and a shame
that it happened to that family,
but I truly believed it
could never happen to me.
So foolishly young and naive.
Then YOU happened —
so tragic, but beautiful.

It started with a smile and a
simple, "Hey."
I soon learned quickly after,
I wasn't immune to BETRAYAL.

Everyday the reality
is that you don't care
that my heart longs for you
to want me,
and for me
to be good enough;
PRETTY ENOUGH.

I always smile
a certain smile at you
in hopes that in my happiness
you'd see exactly what you do to me.

If I was a hurricane,
you would be the
EYE OF MY STORM.

But though I daydream of a love
that may never be true,
I meet you in my dreams,
where there, you love me.
How sweet it would be
if you could just see how perfect
we are together
inside my mind's slumber.

He vexed me
the way each word
rolled off his tongue,
as if angels placed them there
to be delicately delivered.
His eyes perfectly symmetrical,
his hair, luscious.
He was the perfect storm
of TEMPTATION and BLISS

Oh how I yearned for one kiss from
the boy that was OUT OF MY LEAGUE.

Life has gotten heavy recently,
like the weight of the fall leaves
after it rains.
Or maybe it's my tears
that make the ground so weighed down.

I turn to the sky
and I'm quickly reminded of why
there's hope.
It's spilt out across the sky,
like a painting by Monet.

I must say, the orange and purple
left at the horizon is the beauty
that calms my heart.

As the sun rises and falls,
so do MY FEARS of it all.

I fell in love with
your BAD BOY ways —
the way you lusted for me,
and touched me,
as if I was the very first girl.
When in reality,
I probably wasn't even the first that day.
But you had a way of
making me believe I was invincible
when we were together.

You were an outcast from HEAVEN,
and I loved the taste of SIN ON YOUR LIPS

You were an outcast
from Heaven,
and I loved the taste of

𝔰𝔦𝔫

on your lips.

I now know why we were taught
as children to never play with fire.

A spark like ours
turned into an explosion.
Our fates were CHOSEN,
burnt by loves DEVOTION,
our futures set in MOTION.

We will burst into something
beautiful together,
for I always favored
fire over ice.

Though any version of
FOREVER with you will suffice.

I'm not scared of you
breaking my heart.
I've been hurt before,
but I never allow anything
to break me
that isn't meant for me.

Though that took years
of being strong
and looking deep inside myself
for strength,
the only thing I actually
FEAR
in this ill-fated world is
never getting the
chance to LOVE YOU.

I have endlessly been the girl
everybody falls in love with
so quickly.

The first conversation
that turns into lust,
and endless nights of building trust.

But the more you get to know
my depth,
the more intimidating I become.

I've learned that
the girl who is DEEP,
that loves with her heart on her sleeve,
is the girl whose aura shines too bright,
so they LEAVE.

Our love will still haunt me tomorrow,
because goodbye was never my idea.
Yet a cruel fate
made me watch you
turn your back.

And while these walls absorb my pain,
and start to crack,
I sit here and wish LOVE
was enough to make you STAY.

The sun,
now at the break of the
horizon.
As darkness falls,
so do my hopes of it all.
(My hopes that your lies
are NOT just lies.)
Convincing myself,
"He truly tries."

So as I lay in a field of
dandelions and confusion,
I make a wish
that when DARKNESS falls,
so will peace,
and so will my perspective
of YOU; of it all.

And though writing a poem to you
would be a beautiful way
to express the magnitude of my love
for you,
I realize I can't express, through mere words,
the true passion and devotion
I have for you.

LOVE isn't always describable through words.
I tried to convey it in every language, but nowhere
in this world did I find the words to match this feeling.

I felt through one look, it's the type of love
that goes beyond any realm.
Poets try to describe it,
yet can't explain the actual magnitude of it;
the type of love that is FELT,
not heard, or seen.
It's the way I know
every second of everyday
my love for you is undeniably one of
the worlds greatest wonders.

With no words to explain how,
I know with my entire being,
you BELONG with me.

"Why did you decide to bear it all?"

Because I didn't know who I was
before the fall;
before he took my soul and
ripped it wide open,
in attempt to build himself a home.

Now I know,
I'd rather be alone than to appease a fake love.

She's as MESSED UP as can be,
HER MIND is a tangled ball of yarn,
and she has RAW BEAUTY like no other.

She's the kind of girl
guys turn away from,
because she's a lot to handle.
But he stayed to tame her fears,
and untie her mind.

He loved the challenge that she was,
because never has a woman's mind left him so
WONDERSTRUCK.

He saw the demons
of my past
and exorcised them,
one at a time.

Every trauma, slain,
as if he were the PRINCE
on the white horse that
they talk about in fairytales.
Or maybe he was
a little bit of heaven
here on earth.

All I know is he gave me
back my hope,
and showed me
my worth.

Either way,
I PRAY he stays.

I need to be CLEANSED of you.
BAPTIZED in water you've yet to
corrupt with the evil you so
mercilessly throw at things —
things that should
only be touched with

purity.

I hope when you see me with him
your BLOOD boils;
that the sight of his lips
touching mine makes you recoil.

This will be your fate for your sins —
dreading everyday,
reliving the inescapable affliction
you will feel
for every infidelity
you thought you committed
surreptitiously.

I hope the TEMPTATION was worth it.

It's not the tears I've cried
or the years that I've spent
trying to justify
your actions,
when you continuously showed me
you would never change,
but my loyalty that kept me there for years.
I yearned to be enough for you,
and for you to see what we had built
and not rush to tear it all down;
for my **BLOOD, SWEAT**, and **TEARS**
to finally pay off.
I wished for you to choose me.
Instead, my youth was wasted
because of the sins you tasted.

I **NEVER** should have stayed.
Because of your insecurities, you betrayed,
and now I can never get back those years.

A fable fib
became a tale as old as time.
I didn't see the crime.
I was blinded by beauty,
so gallantly alluring;
my tears pouring.
I should have been more wise.
PRINCE CHARMING
only saved
the princess
because he had his own
KINGDOM in his eyes.

I should have been
more wise.
PRINCE CHARMING
only saved the princess
because he had his own

𝕶𝖎𝖓𝖌𝖉𝖔𝖒

in his eyes.

Free me from this
BEAUTIFUL LIE.
Deny me the pleasure
your secret betrayal
causes.

Leave me in my MADNESS
to bathe in tears of sorrow,
knowing the "truest" moments
of my life, were in fact fraud.

I fell hard for your SCHEMES.
Now the denial of the truth
will be my demise.

Our love burnt the same color orange
as the trees on the mountain side,
in an aesthetically BEAUTIFUL way.

We changed as gently,
and as bravely
as the last fighting embers
on a cold night.

Like the seasons,
we were also FALLING SLOWLY.

Shame pulses through my heart —
the warmth is fading.
Your love, though sinful, is sedating.
Each touch leaves me intoxicated.
Though wrong, I need more;
my soul, at war, with no one keeping score.
I knew what I was in for.

You were UNHOLY but you
made me feel WHOLE.

You were

unholy

but you made me feel

whole.

I will be cursed for eternity —
cursed to find you each lifetime,
fall endlessly in love with every inch of you,
every misfortune,
and trauma you carry…
just to have you ripped away
repeatedly.
Cursed to feel
the horror of
HEARTBREAK and GOODBYES.
Cursed by these intrusive memories
that plague my mind.
(A time when we were
once playful, carefree, young,
in love, and happy.)

Now the oath to evil
another took in jealousy
has DAMNED me
to watched you be ripped away
endlessly.

He was a living Alcatraz,
trapped on an island
of his own misery.

His soul was HAUNTED
by each tormented heart
he abused throughout the years.

You can hear their TEARS,
and SCREAMS of SORROW
echoed throughout time.

Oh what a cruel fate
that waits him,
for the injustice
of each girl he victimized
along the way.

Echoes of
HAUNTING memories
engulf me.
Chaotic symphonies
play their last call.

I dedicated my life to you,
I gave you MY ALL.

Now I dedicate
this last melody
as the seasons change,
like the bare branches on a lonely tree,
waiting the arrival of new leaves.

I'll wish upon a dandelion
that you grow back to LOVING ME.

Your memory
weighs me down,
like I carry the weight
of your sins.
We
were
as different as
FIRE and LIGHTENING,
but what we had in common
is we were both dangerous,
yet equally beautiful.
It's as if we were once the same,
TWO OPPOSITES;
half of one another.

I will carry your memory
as we part,
knowing
in each and every lifetime,
somehow FATE will place me
back into your arms.

Bare branches,
bare skin;
sheets wrinkle like the leaves
that blanket the ground.
The air turns colder
as you hold her.
Falling into you
she now knows
why AUTUMN
is her favorite season.

She was indestructible
in every way.
With hell fire burning,
and a crooked halo,
she was a HEAVENLY paradox.

An angel with flames,
whose love could truly set you ablaze
in heavenly bliss.

She was all for him.

As they laid in a bed of sin,
he got a taste of
both HEAVEN and HELL.
Each sip went down so well.

I slipped holy water
on your tongue
in hopes of purifying your words.
Instead your tongue caught FIRE.
You turned into and inconceivable LIAR.
The idle-promises,
the deception.
Not to mention,
each moment I thought was real
was mere mockery.
(Moments I cherished.)

It's now hard to grasp that
something that felt so good
was so fake.

You wanted to fight.
I wasn't in the mood.
Sorry if you thought it was rude
that I walked away,
but the wind had picked up
and I already felt the chill of unspoken hurt.

As you conjure up these false conclusions,
I'll be in my bed weeping,
with the moonlight tucking in my sorrows.

I'll never understand the allure
of always having to argue.
Just remember, I WIN IN THE END.

For too long
I gave you the pen
to write my story.

You made me the casualty,
and you wrote yourself
as the main character of my life.
Now I'm taking back what's mine,
and re-writing the part you left behind —
the part where you left me in pain.

I will now be the author of my own life
and tell the story that's meant to be told,
(the one where I SAVE MYSELF.)

You say you'll cross oceans for me,
yet I'm the one willing
to become
the entire ocean
if it means always being surrounded by you.

YOU'RE MY LAND
(safe, beautiful, and serene.)
AS I AM YOUR SEA,
(unpredictable and chaotic.)

Together our love is stronger than
the currents
I fight to get to you.

You called me your angel,
ripped off my wings,
then demanded me to fly.
I never asked why,
attempting to do right by you,
for the sake of loyalty.

But once touched with
WICKED HANDS,
I was no longer pure.

I'll never forget
the day someone asked of me,
"Was the POISON
you ingested to earn his LOVE
worth the pain you're enduring now?"

You left me staring out that same window,
watching you turn your back on me.

Every time you would
get in the car and drive away,
you would take my hopes
and my every ill-fated oath.

I watched each dream shatter,
as I shattered the glass,
in attempt to see clearer.
But all I managed to see
was the devastation
you neglectfully left behind.
Blood dripping from my hand,
each drop
dripping the memory of a time
you told me you'd never leave.
(A puddle of DECEPTION.)

I now see
my broken reflection,
thanks to the words,
"I'll never leave you."

I knew the day would come
when a girl would catch your eye.
And I definitely can't lie,
I have been in denial of this day
since our last goodbye.

I don't want to see her,
because I don't want to try to compare
what you see in her and not me.
That's NOT FAIR.

But one thing I have learned
is that the love
I hold in my heart for you,
it's pure.
Because though I had our future
mapped out in my mind,
I still somehow find the courage
to wish you blessings.

I wish you BLISS.
And in this,
I realize there's something
beatific in maturing.

Today I decided
to forgive you.
Not because YOU'RE SORRY,
because we all know YOU'RE NOT.
But because I see the despise
you hold for yourself
in your eyes;
the monster you see in the mirror.
So I'll forgive the lies.
You were the one HURTING
all along, not me.

I see the destruction
in your eyes.
I see the end of days portrayed,
lurking in the
DARKNESS
of your pupils.
I see meteors
raining down
in a bright,
but unfortunate DOOM.
But with a kiss so enthralling,
if our love brings
on the end,
I'll be there WITH YOU.
As the sun engulfs
the earth,
as long as your warmth
is the last thing I feel.

I altered FATE
and changed REALITY,
because even the mere thought
of being without you
is a travesty.

I may be punished
for these actions,
but the biggest punishment of all
would be every second
I would not be next to you.

I will take on HEAVEN and freeze HELL.
I will burn the devil at a stake,
all if anyone tried
to take you from me.
And this may seem insane,
but when it comes to your happiness,
I can never be detained
from doing anything and everything
to give you the happy ending that you deserve.

The leaves started falling,
and the dying embers
weren't keeping me warm,
for my soul was yearning
for a love, worthy.
I felt loneliness,
but didn't want to confuse
just any closeness
with comfort.
I craved something genuine
something authentically
sent from above.

I craved TRUE love.

I will fight for you
and become the darkness
all to have you to myself.

I will become the
　　　CREATURE of NIGHTMARES
all to give you your dreams.

I will walk through realities,
choose your happiest moments
and make sure you live consistently
in every one of your favorite memories.
I will be THE VILLAIN
in everyone else's story,
as long as I am the HERO in yours.
For you, there is absolutely nothing
I won't do.
Our love,
　　　though tortured,
　　　　　will be TRUE.

After being with you,
there would be
no such thing
as normal ever again.
You left me DISORIENTED,
IN LOVE,
and DESPERATE for your affection.

I'm so tired of being the one
who FEELS more,
and the one who LOVES harder.
The one always carrying your burdens,
yearning,
begging for the love
that you give
everyone else but me.

Am I wrong to feel broken
by love?
Because you're right here,
yet I still can't reach you.
I can crawl,
but even at your knees,
you enjoy looking down at me.
Look up instead,
that's your only chance at redemption.

The temptation was so alluring,

I confused **love** with **lust,**

and **desire** for **destiny.**

You played the cards against me
so I took the cards you dealt,
sliced myself open
and bled out
every lie.
But the jokes on YOU.
Though
BLEEDING and BROKEN,
I will win
in the end,
and my wounds,
they will HEAL.

Your eyes,
like a pool of HONEY
and CHESNUT,
swirling
like the CINNAMON
in my latte.
Your lips as sweet
as dripping icing.
Your aura,
enticing.
One sip of you is all it took.
You are now my FAVORITE flavor.

If another love is what you seek then
always CHOOSE HER, shamelessly.
You may change my outlook on love,
but I'd rather you choose someone else
over settling for a love that doesn't consume you.
Because even if I am found hysterical, on the floor,
searching for my sanity, I soon will find my pride.
And even though your existence will still taunt my
entire being, I will find enough of myself to
remember who I was before your touch confused me.
Though I'll have my moments of weakness,
I won't break.
I'll shatter BEAUTIFULLY.

And even though your existence
will still taunt my entire being,
I will find enough of myself to
remember who I was before
your touch

𝔠𝔬𝔫𝔣𝔲𝔰𝔢𝔡 𝔪𝔢.

Though I'll have my moments
of weakness, I won't break.
I'll shatter

𝔟𝔢𝔞𝔲𝔱𝔦𝔣𝔲𝔩𝔩𝔶.

You waged war on a love
that has already won
countless victories.
You thought of me as weak
because I hold
a dignified and graceful way about myself
that confused you —
distracting you from the
savage blood I carry,
from my ancestors
who perfected the ART of WAR.

One thing I know for sure,
if you try to interfere
with a love I hold dear,
I'll become your
WORST NIGHTMARE.

It's not our LAST GOODBYE
that I dwell on,
but our FIRST HELLO.

Little did I know,
that would be the moment
I'd crave to go back to
for the rest of my life.

You looked at me that night
like I was the only thing that existed
in the world;
like in tales of lovers;
like you were crossing the sea
just to reach me.
That night,
I WAS YOUR OCEAN.

I've never favored fairytales,
nor truly believed in a happy ending.
There's something **BEAUTIFUL**
about a love so tragic
it breaks you down
to your very core,
craving to hear more.
A love so strong
it reaches through all realms,
and is recognized in every lifetime.
I guess that's why
I've always chased **DISASTER,**
subconsciously
looking for a love
too strong for this world.

I was once told,
"I'd rather you cry now
then the rest of your life."
But how can anyone foresee
a fate so cruel
over a bad moment
in both of our lives.

Though LOVE is strong,
so is the DEMON of DISASTER.

He violently
created chaos
in both of our lives,
trying to break our love apart.
I just wasn't strong enough to fight
both of our demons at the same time.
We knew these demons from the start,
and a "rough patch' isn't a toxic relationship,
it's real life.

It DOESN'T define our love.
Because I can tell you this,
we will never be understood
in a generation that thrives
on finding beauty in all that is fake.

Shower me in RAINDROPS.
I have survived
too many storms
to be scared of your
HURRICANE of emotions.
I grew to love the way
each raindrop feels,
as if it hits me
and purifies the words left on my skin.

I'll turn your tropical storm into a
BLIZZARD
and leave you understanding
why the cold has always intrigued you.

I will LOVE YOU past death.
So the day that I take my last breath,
rejoice on my grave;
know
that our love
will awaken my spirit
and I will eternally dance with you.
I'll be grateful for the gift
of being your ghost.
When the scriptures spoke:
"I am with you ALWAYS,"
that was God also speaking
our love into EVERY EXISTENCE;
EVERY REALM.

I never realized
the oceans you were willing to cross
to get to me.
I knew your LOVE was strong,
and true,
but as I sat at the coast
waiting for your arrival,
you were taking on
fierce winds and unforgivable currents,
all to reach me.

I couldn't wait to hold you in my arms,
but days became months,
and our love became a tragic shipwreck
somewhere in the deep dark sea.
You were still stuck on the voyage
to get home to me.

So I'll take on the same waves
and search each inch
of the ocean floor,
til' you are in my arms once more.
I'll accept whatever fate I need too, to find you.
Because home was never a place.
Home was YOU.

One day we shall roam
the earth
floating inches above the ground,
DANCING upon the seas,
as we sway over waves,
and sit on the clouds.
So even on the cloudiest of nights
we will have endless starry nights.
Oh how beautiful it will be to finally be free.
We will travel through walls,
scare the living,
leaving them telling stories of
STAR-CROSSED lovers
who still cross over the realms to
roam the earth together.

I want nothing more
than to be the GHOST STORY
of the two who loved each other into death.

Hold onto my touch.
I've missed you way too much.
I didn't realize how fast time goes,
but I promise from this moment on,
I'll be there for you.
Through your
HIGHS and LOWS
and the moments
impulse seems to take control.
I'll be there to calm your mind,
so lets make up for lost time.
COLLIDING twice
is not a coincidence,
but our sign.
You were meant for me
like a heavenly law created,
stating that
our spirits will be
FOREVER intertwined.

Since you left,
I have been searching for you
in someone else —
longing to feel the passion
and soul consuming
feeling of your kiss, from those
PERFECT LIPS.
But the harder I try to move on
and be with someone new
the more I have learned
no one will ever TASTE LIKE YOU.

Days turned into weeks,
and weeks turned into years,
searching through tears.
I finally decided,
I'm done scavenging
through your heart
to find love.
I'd rather be left STARVING.

I was dipped like a
strawberry in a
CHOCOLATE
flavored despair.
You had no intention to be with me,
yet you hated to share.
I thought you cared.
Shame on me,
I ended up being
just another girl you tasted.
Though it wasn't time wasted,
only lessons learned,
I was too sweet for your
DARK WAYS.

I have been avoiding the real question.
Is there something wrong with me
for LOVING a man like you?

I call you A MONSTER,
yet when you show your fangs,
I can only but crave for you to sink your teeth
deep into me and TASTE ME.
Swallow me.
Devour me in your sin.

I'd travel all of hell if
I knew you were there waiting for me.

I don't know if darkness is my DESTINY,
or if I'm chasing something that's going to
leave me a skeleton of who I was…
but I do know I have never felt
more alive than I do in your SHADOW.

Orange clouds engulfing the sky,
a gentle kiss GOODBYE,
light rain falls down
and washes my sorrows away.
I pleaded to the universe,
let him stay…
but lust got in the way.
And my heart,
you did betray.
I'm afraid to let go,
though I know the day has come.
I hope in time
you NEVER FORGET ME.

I let a boy create my
DEPRESSION,
and here's my confession:
He broke me into pieces
and it's fucking with me mentally.
I gave him my all
and he broke me in two.
It was all A GAME,
A LIE,
NEVER TRUE.

I wish I knew he promised me
forever with fingers crossed behind his back.
Only a monster could do that.

Like his lies, his soul turned BLACK.

He had no compassion;
decency he lacked.
I packed my bags.
This time I'm never looking back.
I gave him too much power, and
that was my mistake from the start.
This is now where we PART.

These TATTOOS I have
are so much more than just INK.
They are letters to you
I wear on my skin.
It tells in a single portrait,
along with every single word,
that I carry you with me always,
for the world to see.

LIKE DIAMONDS,
I wear you with pride.

She's a bit much —
unpredictable and defiant.
Yet that chaos that rages in her soul
is what sets your heart ablaze.
She is different in a uniquely beautiful way.
Loving her unleashes a part of you,
and it grows to be your favorite part.
GIRLS LIKE HER,
you CAN'T CAGE their emotions,
and taming them would be a sin.
Because loving everything she is
made you everything you
now fearlessly are.

Girls like her,
you can't cage their
emotions,
and taming them
would be a sin.
Because loving
everything she is
made you everything
you now

𝕱𝕖𝖆𝖗𝖑𝖊𝖘𝖘𝖑𝖞 are.

Your delusions,
while intriguing,
were such a
PRETTY POISON to digest.
But while beautiful,
it had disaster written all over it…
and still I DEVOURED them
like SUNDAY MORNING COFFEE —
warm going down,
with the inevitability
of regret.

When we first met,
flowers grew out of the grief I carried.
My sorrow was buried
and I was REBORN,
like rose buds in the spring,
while nature sung to the joy of rebirth,
and all that it brings.
I too grew from your love,
from your warmth,
like you were my sun bringing me
back to something BEAUTIFUL.
And though you reminded me
of who I truly was,
I have to remember,
spring and summer are short lived,
and the cold always come
creeping slowly back in.

Our last goodbye
was the first time
I ever truly saw THE REAL YOU —
the 'YOU' that you hid
or I BLINDLY chose not to see.

It took making and breaking love
for your true colors to show.
   Your lips left SCARS.

I was suffocating behind your lies,
now I am finally free
of the loveless melody you hummed.

We get tangled in LIFE,
LOVE,
and HEARTBREAK,
in the search of a happily ever after.

We completely wrap ourselves
in a web of lies
on what love is supposed to be,
that by the time we find true love
standing right in front of us,
we are entwined by expectation,
and are too blinded
to even see what we could've had.

I know our LOVE.
I know THE TYPE.
The souls undeniably made for each other,
recognizable in any lifetime; any realm.
The two souls that
merge into ONE
and roam this strange world together,
realizing their bodies are only holding their spirits.
It's a safe haven for their flames,
to use and to learn,
to grow in love.

But here without YOURS,
mine will slowly wither.
We will not have to be like
those stories of love suicides,
because without you next to me,
my body,
it will SLOWLY DIE.

It will be ready to encompass
the next journey to wherever you are.

You're just a mere echo
of a HAPPY MEMORY
etched into my mind.
I replay it when life gets quiet.

A memory from so long ago
that reminds me life
wasn't always this hard,
nor did I carry grief as heavy
as I do now.

I remember being CAREFREE
and not knowing what it was like
to have someone ripped away from me.

Now I find solace
all these years later
by keeping you stored in my mind,
where I can always find you
when I NEED YOU.

I broke my own heart
along the way to finding you,
with unreal expectations
and experiences
that left me in tears.
So I sit here and try to blame you
for this pain in my heart.
But the truth is, it's been building up
long before we ever met.
You probably decided to walk away
because I chase disappointment.

Sometimes I think my soul seeks out
heartbreak just to feel more DEEPLY.

I never needed to be saved.
I found the strength within me to save myself.
I needed a LOVE that would awaken a part of my
soul not yet ignited; a LOVE gentle enough to
reinforce to me that the safe haven I already built
for myself will remain secure.
I yearn for that someone that will always help
keep us both SAFE.

I carry our love encased in my heart,
entombed in concrete, you and I will
NEVER part.
When I die, bury me under a blanket
of wilted white roses and visit me at night,
for I have always felt more solace in the
absence of light.
But I do pray I see his face at first light.
I only want to be ANYWHERE he is.
Uncage our love and let eternity set us free.

I only want to be

𝖆𝖓𝖞𝖜𝖍𝖊𝖗𝖊 he is.

This pain,
this gut wrenching,
soul sucking void
you feel,
this unbearable feeling in your chest,
it will in time
loosen it's grasp on you.

You will be able EVENTUALLY
to BREATHE
more EFFORTLESSLY.

Tangled in sadness and tethered in hope,
you walked away and I'm trying my hardest to cope.
My feelings all intertwine, and though I know the
difference between right and wrong, I know with you
is where I don't belong. I just don't want to face the
truth. I want to hold onto hope. But when I messaged
you to see if you needed anything, you left me on read
and then said 'nope.' As if I wasn't even enough for
you to ask how I was, or even worse, answer me when
I asked how you were, just because of how much I
care. Oh, but how little you do.
I only know I would've given everything to you. I now
have learned that the hope I cling to is not for you to
love me, but for me to FORGET loving you.

He spread his pain around
because it was too much for him
to bear alone.
All his insecurities, shown.
He inflicted his pain on others,
leaving a trail of
mentally drained LOVERS.

There is something about DEJA VU
and every time I look at you,
the way that I feel as if every look
was already taken.
Maybe I'm mistaken,
but I think you were once mine
in another lifetime.
Because I hear your soul calling out to mine,
in hopes it'll quickly recognize
the love we had never died.
It leaves me longing for you once more.
This moment is FATE.
It's where DEJA VU is really just a moment
I was already destined to share with you.

I chased YOU as I chased SUNSETS.
I followed your beauty,
knowing I needed to absorb every ounce
of your intangible essence
before the last of the hues
drew apart from the horizon;
before the last of you was gone.
I knew I was only supposed to enjoy you
for an instant,
but what a mark that moment left
on my soul.
It captured each COLOR of you.

He was TROUBLE,
not the bad kind,
but the fun kind
that would turn your life upside down,
leaving your heart pounding,
intoxicated by the thrill,
screaming for more.
He was tattooed from head to toe,
with a bad boy glare.
When you looked his way
you couldn't help but stare.
He was the boy your body
yearned for,
yet your mind couldn't comprehend.
He was a masterpiece of TRAGEDY.
And I was swimming in sin,
ready to drown in regrets,
over such beautiful eyes.

I wonder if she smells me on your sheets,
or when she kisses you,
can taste the deceit.
How naive can she be
not to see BETRAYAL written in your eyes?
I saw it instantly in our last goodbye,
yet I still tried
to see any good that may be left in you.
But all you did was remind me
to always listen to my intuition.
I already knew you were going
to be the boy that DISAPPOINTED me,
and yet I still,
in your web of lies,
tangled in tears,
tried to find the good somewhere
hiding deep inside you.

I was cursed the minute I saw you.
My life would never be the same.
My fate became heartbreak,
and my nights became echoes of screams.
I shrieked in hopes of releasing some
of this darkness
flowing quickly through my veins.
The moment you walked away
I became an angry, bitter, version of myself,
(my only CURE being you.)
And yet this world fights to keep us apart.

You called me to come to you,
and like always I came running.
And while you see that as a weakness,
it's actually my greatest strength.
It's LOYALTY.
Something you only have for yourself.
So I understand your confusion at my anger,
when the person I'm supposed to know best,
after a night together, acts like we never met.

There will be a part of me missing forever.
Since you left, there is a void carved into my being.
I try to fill it in with people, places, and things,
but I will never quite be able to. The closest I will
come to filling it will be the times that
I am drenched in DAYDREAMS
of my memories OF YOU.

He was a MESS to everyone —
the boy labeled with 'ISSUES.'
Yet when I first laid eyes on him,
I saw the beauty buried
beneath the heartbreak.
I saw a challenge,
yet I already knew the outcome
was going to blow everyone's mind.
I had faith in him from the moment I met him,
and I never faltered in my feelings or my actions.
I looked past the peering eyes
and I only saw him.
He was MISUNDERSTOOD,
but his soul was pure.
I wasn't even sure if I deserved him.

I envied her, and not for the sake of jealously but because not only did you choose her, but she wore you proudly, and with no ill-fated purpose. Just genuine happiness. You wrapped yourself around her life a fur coat in the middle of winter, so everyone could see her beauty. And it was the love you shared with her that I envied, for the mere reason I had never felt it. I also never considered myself beautiful enough to be shown off. But seeing you two together ignited some sort of fire in me. I just want to feel what the two of you have.If even only for a night, I want to know what it feels like to be cherished.

I know I've caused you pain.
I'm not one to deny my misdeeds,
but when I look into your eyes
I see a love so grand.
And though nothing lasts forever,
I'm sorry for every moment
I made you feel unloved.
IT HAUNTS ME.
You've always mattered,
never think you didn't.
Your heart is so pure.
I wasn't sure what I did to deserve you,
but you stayed through all my games.
So if I can leave you with anything,
it's you were the most beautiful thing
I ever destroyed.

If I can leave you

with anything,

it's you were

the most

beautiful

thing I ever

destroyed.

We play a dangerous game when your body touches mine. We laugh it off like we're having fun, and say it'll be fine. But maybe it won't, and we are crossing the line. You kiss my shoulder and suddenly I'm blind to the affliction. I sit there feeling your fingers tracing places that are UNHOLY, believing maybe being seduced by darkness might actually be okay. Though my heart says you're bad, my body is like a puppet on strings. I follow your every command, even if I'm doomed. I'll admit, it feels good to be DAMNED.

I'm not bulletproof,
and words can hurt
as much as bullets,
so take your shot,
but aim correctly.
Because what doesn't kill you
makes you stronger right?
And I hope if there's something
you'll never forget, it's this —
I don't miss, nor do I have **MERCY.**
Maybe it's the curse I carry in my cold soul,
or the blessing of strength
passed down to me from generations
of my ancestors —
learning their greatest mistakes,
and wanting better for their children.
Either way,
I pray you know what you're starting
before you beg for mercy,
because you didn't know
who you were messing with.

When OUR LOVE dies,
I will bury it beneath the dirt
and mark it with a tree,
in hopes in our next lifetime
we come across it together and see —
for thousands of lifetimes,
in each,
you ALWAYS find your way back to me.

I have always been able to deal with heartache gracefully. I've never begged nor pleaded. I was already being pushed to an edge. Why make it worse? Instead, I've just accepted it and expressed my pain in private, crying in the shower with loud music to hide my tears. I'm the kind of girl that will walk in the rain, just to sob uncontrollably. But just because I don't beg or cry to be kept by someone willing to let me go, doesn't mean it doesn't HURT.

You're as TOXIC as the air
after a raging fire,
yet you cloud my mind.
I can't ESCAPE,
so I continuously breathe you in,
despite knowing you will
take my breath AWAY.

I feel it TRAGIC that you do not understand
my broken heart. What broke it was immense love
and pure happiness. Because without these things,
you can't feel heartbreak. While you see that as a gift,
I see it as a PUNISHMENT; an injustice you're doing
to yourself. You're shielding yourself from something
blissful over the mere thought you might get hurt.
The only tragedy I see is never getting to know a
love so true.

I ran to the hiding place in my mind.
I needed a moment to escape this world.
I guess he did too.
He was sitting in my thoughts.
He looked up, smiling, saying:
 "I hope you don't mind sharing."

That's the moment I knew
the VISION of HIM, alone,
was enough to calm my racing mind.

NOVEMBER is a month I'll always remember.
As I sit here and reminisce, I tremble. While everyone
is giving thanks, I sit in a room full of people and stare
at the chair you'd usually fill, NOW EMPTY, holding
the ghost of your memory. I'm longing to know where
you are, who you're with, and whose family's chair
you are filling now. I sit by the fire and I hear their
laughs from your jokes, in my head.
(The same ones you told my family.)
I don't want to long for you anymore or search for you
in a room of crowded people, but as I go to give
thanks this holiday, I seem to always be grateful for
every moment I spent with you. It's true, I can't let go
of you. Wherever you now are, I wonder if you're
thinking of me too.

I'm thankful for
the heartbreak
that came of you.
I would have never seen
true love
without it.
So I give thanks
to your dishonor,
and cherish the love
it brought me.
I now know when you
lose one thing,
it's possible it's because
there is something
BETTER
destined for you.

I wonder if she sees the pain in your eyes,
or has caught onto your lies.
Or are you hiding them all too well?
I know your scars and the despise you hold inside
from past mistakes that you carry in your
subconscious.
I know you too well.
Because while falling in love with your soul,
I introduced myself to your mind,
and in time I grew to love you.
(The tortured soul at war with himself, constantly.)
But let me confess,
I do hurt less knowing
she'll never LOVE YOU like I do.

The dark STORM CLOUDS remind me of you.
There is something sinister about the way they come
on so fast, filling the sky with DARKNESS —
the same way you came into my life,
leaving a void in my heart.
Yet the rain is soothing, and the noise calms my
chaotic mind for a moment, reminding me of why
your darkness has always been so intriguing.
It was a high you left me coming down from.
Then on days like today, pouring rain, soothing yet
transparent. You were an intoxicant.
I crave even just a taste of you.
Now I'm left remembering the storm
you stirred in my soul.

Now I'm left
remembering the

𝔰𝔱𝔬𝔯𝔪

you stirred in my soul.

You are MY FOREVER.
So as I lay here on a cold night,
the quietness calms my soul
as I whisper, "Can I keep you?
Can I keep you in all lifetimes, in any form,
in every possible way unseen to the human eye;
incomprehensible to the human mind.
Can I keep you ALWAYS?"

Promise you'll come to me haunt me.
Terrorize me. Leave me wondering
where my sanity has run off to.
Because in the end, if I get to keep your love,
I will keep it in any way that I can have it.
Let our love possess me in a way
I can be everywhere with you.
Let me keep you ALWAYS.

Let our love possess me in a way
I can be everywhere with you.
Let me keep you

always.

You ravished through me
like a **WILD FIRE**
hungers for a **FOREST**;
like a **QUEEN WASP**
surviving the
FROZEN WINTER.

Fighting for life,
you put your all into
DESTROYING me.
Your false love is the
one thing I need protection from,
yet the only thing
I don't know how to save myself from.

My heart is FROZEN.
As I exhale condensation,
it surrounds me in a fog —
clouded and confused of how you
got away with saying our love was true.
I believed you when you spoke all the words
that now pierce my heart as ice.
But I'm not the girl
to make the same mistake twice.
Keep my WARMTH,
you'll need it where you're going.
I found comfort in the COLD.

It was the beginning of DECEMBER,
and I remember our love grew stronger
as we laid, entangled in our sheets,
as beautiful as the quilted white snow
that covered the streets.
Worries laid to rest with
your head
on my chest.
I felt your breath warm.
It was a serendipitous moment.

You are the only proof I will ever need to know angels walk this earth. You are HEAVEN in every form, yet this world tainted you, and the darkness that stains everything unfortunately reached you,
leaving you, a piece of HEAVEN, here hurting.
I too have been touched by the stain. So take the light I have since then acquired, and cast out the dark in you. If my fate is to save you, build yourself a safe haven inside of my soul. I'll die with a smile and reunite with you when the time is right.

I looked at a snowman
and watched as a single tear
fell from his eye.
I don't know how he was able
to foresee our soon to be goodbye.
Maybe he too felt he was built upon LIES.
But I can't deny,
I'm grateful that he left me with that sign.
I was able to cherish the moment a little longer,
while I grew stronger,
getting ready for the inevitable.
As the sun and the snowman slowly died,
our love remained FROZEN
in the MEMORIES OF WINTER.

As the

sun

and the

snowman

slowly died,
our love remained
frozen
in the memories of
winter.

I love the way the snow
covers everything after a blizzard.
It blankets all my indiscretions
in a pure white cloak.
You and me,
all around serene,
as the moonlight creates sparkles,
like tiny diamonds
scattered across fields of lust.
I know loving you is wrong,
but the wind is carrying our song.
Your lips, cold, need my warmth.
I'll build an igloo just for us two —
where even if only for a night
I get to be your SNOW ANGEL.

Your lips,
cold,
need my warmth.
I'll build an igloo
just for us two —
where even if
only for a night,
I get to be your

𝔰𝔫𝔬𝔴

𝔞𝔫𝔤𝔢𝔩.

We shattered like an
ornament falling off the
CHRISTMAS TREE —
so fast we couldn't grasp
it was even happening.
But our love came smashing down,
our scattered memories shattered all around.
For a minute everything was quiet
and there was no sound.
The way we broke was profound.
Now, left lonely, I will pick up each piece as these
feelings are swept away.
You were gone before I even got the chance
to ask you to STAY.

Blood red engulfed the skies.
I truly tried,
but each lie grew larger.
Like a puddle of blood
I was sliding in,
trying to escape,
trapped.
Covered in your crimson deceit,
I finally retreated.
I was stuck in a MONSTER'S grip.
As the blood drips,
and I shed each layer left of you,
I am no longer your victim.

The ghost of CHRISTMAS' past
stopped by in a frozen frenzy,
to remind me that we didn't last.
As I was shown reels of our favorite
moments flashing ever so fast,
my heart dropped,
the torture of this season,
I pray will stop.
As I lie melancholy alone under the mistletoe,
the only gift I pray for is to forget how you made
every CHRISTMAS cozy.
I can no longer feel
the warmth of the fire,
I am FROZEN inside.

You looked at me and instinctively said, "just leave."
Sobbing, I held onto you, clinging, asking why you
said, "I'm doing this for you." As if the heartache you
were causing me was unpretentious. As if leaving me
was ever an option. I have already danced with your
demons in flames and I have taken them as my own…
so you're not protecting me from something I already
intimately know. I applaud your choice to try and
keep me safe, but without you is not an option I'd ever
even consider. So I will wear your love on my skin,
and battle your wars within.
I would NEVER be okay without you.

You were the PERFECT STORM —
tall, dark, and handsome,
but profoundly fierce, just as a BLIZZARD.
Mesmerizing, like the white snow
falling and swirling in harsh winds.
You caught me off guard.
You knocked me off my feet,
as dangerous as sleet.
I went seeking shelter,
sliding right into you.
And what a beautiful safe haven you've been.

I have been making excuses for a man who has
continuously broken my heart over and over.
Cheating, then denying it.
All the things I already knew to be true,
trying to make me feel less of a woman,
thinking he'll get away with it if he directs it on me,
saying, "It's your "insecurities."
It's always been the same old song,
all his sins on repeat.
He sucks the energy right out of me.
I just need to accept defeat, because you can't win
against someone who is never willing to admit their
wrongs.

I can't say goodbye to my sadness,
for it is the only reminder of you
that I can feel so deeply.
So I will hold to it
like a mother cradling a baby,
gentle with no intention of ever letting go.
I do not want to remember a lifetime
without love,
even if those feelings brought pain.
I'd rather go insane, than numb.
I need to remember,
even having the WORST of you
was better then NONE of you.

I hope he makes you feel like the
same magic you felt
the night before CHRISTMAS,
waiting for Santa to bring all your gifts.
You believed in magic then,
and I hope he makes you
believe in it now too.
I hope he brings back that innocence for you.
And I hope that you become his
CHRISTMAS MORNING gift.

As I dream of a WHITE CHRISTMAS,
I also dream of you and how beautiful it
would be to cuddle, cozy by the fire;
how it would feel to encompass peace.
I want the emptiness I carry around to be filled.
I know you and I could be something
uniquely MAGICAL.

If it comes with a price, run for your life.
Not just any love will suffice.
Love does not come with demands.
Love is two imperfect people,
holding hands,
with no expectations, or judgement.
Real love is finally being free,
BUT NOT ALONE.

I wanted to believe you,
but like so many times before
it was never the truth,
just stories you'd fabricate
to get yourself out of being honest.
You knew your love made me weak
and only I could dismiss
the lies in your angel eyes.
And though you'd always get caught,
no matter how hard I tried to say goodbye,
I'd end up being the one lying to myself,
saying, "I can actually leave."
Til' I smelled her on you.
That's when I finally knew I'd find the strength.
But that'd be the LAST TIME
you ever saw me again.

As the ground grows colder
and the dirt freezes over,
I will bury my hopes at midnight,
and remember we were at least
worth a try.
But not everything,
even if it is as
BEAUTIFUL as you and me,
is meant to be for longer
than a season.

There are so many things in life
that were handed to me as presents,
that I wish I never unwrapped.
That paper cut I got that day
was a premonition of the dread
I was gifted,
and the days of sorrow to come.
I never knew my heartache
could reach to certain depths.

And what KILLS ME,
is it was handed to me with a SMILE.

I thought you were my
TWIN FLAME,
but our wick slowly dimmed.
Maybe it was the smell of indecency,
and how you turned me away.
Either way, I was wrong.
You weren't half of me,
only the OPPOSITE.
It was MY FAULT I only saw
what I wished to see.

As I lay staring at the sky,
it let down a single snowflake
from heaven,
landing straight of my cheek,
freezing my tears.
As if the sky itself was saying,
"It's time to let go of
this pain and HEAL.
Darling, it's BEAUTIFUL to feel,
just not for the wrong person."

I say I'm over you,
yet here I am at 2 A.M.,
headphones on,
crying to your FAVORITE SONGS.
I'm not even sure what the words are.
My mind is too clouded to tell.
All I do know is how each lyric brings me back
to a memory when I was happy,
and its been awhile since I've seen that smile.
These songs are all I have —
they bring me back to all that's left of YOU.

He seduced me, cruelly,
with his **BURNING EYES**,
long before the fatal touch
of his **ICE COLD HANDS**
left me yearning to
feel warmth once more.

You asked me how I was
and I replied,
"I'm doing just fine,"
faked a smile,
and held onto your promise
that we would remain friends.
But what I really meant was,
I'm ALIVE...
I'm BREATHING...
but since you left,
your still all I think about.
So I'll pretend,
even tell myself
I'm okay,
just so I never have to
hear you
say a final GOODBYE.

No matter how far you try to run
from heartbreak,
the darkness always follows.
You still have a SHADOW on the moon.

There is this BOY.
He reminds me of someone
I USED TO KNOW.
His eyes carry the same heavy burdens.
Life wasn't easy for him.
He's covered from head to toe in regret,
yet the light that he carries in his soul
is mesmerizing.
The bright aura that draws you in,
because it's intriguing.
He reminds me of a boy I loved.
Maybe that's why I fantasize
every time I see HIS EYES.
Maybe it's because I see the memories I miss,
that I'm dying to relive
just one more time.
Or maybe it's my soul saying,
"You still have so much more to give."
Either way, I'm not exactly sure.
I just know that this boy,
he reminds me so much of somebody
I never truly wanted to let go of.

I will **NEVER REGRET** loving you,
even if it meant losing you.
Love will always conquer even the worst pain.
No matter the way we had to part,
or the way we said goodbye,
I will never regret a single day.
Though I can barely stand the agony,
I choose to remember
I once felt more happiness in a single moment
than all this pain combined.
All I'll ever regret,
is that our love didn't
LAST LONGER.

Our DESTINY was always to
shine bright together,
in our nebula of passion,
as we pulsate in conjunction
with the very STARS
we were made from.

My heart finally froze,
due to all the heartache life has shown.
All the HEARTBREAKS
and PAST TRAUMA.
I froze the roses and flowers
that surrounded me,
in remembrance of the beauty
that once was so alive.
All I can hope is that someday,
someone's warmth will thaw out
the COLD BLIZZARD in my soul.

Cobwebs glistened with the moonlight,
as they were sprinkled with snowflakes,
it reminded me even the most unthoughtful
of things can be unexpectedly BEAUTIFUL.
Calming all my intrusive thoughts,
relaxed, I thought of you and how something so
overlooked can bear so much beauty.
And in that exact moment, I wondered for the first
time in so long, if you still listen to our favorite song.
I then realized it's the small things,
like YOU, I'll always miss.

I remember all the lies you whispered
in my ear. You manifested all my fears.
I never thought I'd say this,
but I never thought I would see
the GOOD in our GOODBYE.
But my heart now shines
differently from the hole
you punctured through it,
it now shines BRIGHTER.

I hope she's holding you right now,
looking into your eyes,
telling you she loves you.
Because I'm 100 miles away,
wishing I was with you,
looking at our pictures
(pictures of times I pretend
I wish to forget)...
praying at the exact moment that
I'm feeling empty, she is making you feel whole.
I hope she loves you the way I always will.
Though our destinies aren't meant to intertwine,
it doesn't mean you
didn't mean THE WORLD to me.

I remember catching snowflakes
with our tongues.
That was the moment the earth was still.
There was MAGIC in the air —
just you and me,
and the snowflakes
we collected as dreams.

You need to feel it sweetheart,
TO HEAL from it.
So don't dodge the words
that shoot like daggers through your heart.
Stand your ground.
What goes around comes around.
Feel it all, then let it go forever.

You and heartbreak DON'T BELONG together.
Like a snowflake would melt in the summer sun,
you and him were DIFFERENT SEASONS.

The night turned cold,
and suddenly I remembered,
you won't be there
to keep me WARM
through the night.
Your side of the bed
now only makes
these nights seem longer.

She cries snowflakes from broken promises,
and creates blizzards from the memory of kisses
her heart misses. Of a love she found a home in.
But like an iceberg floats alone in the dark, desolate
sea, she too was left alone to drift under the stygian
sky, clinging to a memory of what was, and can now
never be.
Something that was once numbingly beautiful

Moving on became tiresome.
I devoted to much of my life
to temporary people,
and I put too much love
into people that didn't deserve me.
I now need to put
the love others turned away
and point it back towards me.
I need to LOVE ME first,
before anyone else
can truly enter this heart of mine.

You are the best parts of a blizzard.
The white swirling, magnificently around;
fiercely.
The same way it all hits so fast
is the same way you knocked me
to my knees.
I sought shelter in you,
from the cold,
and what a BEAUTIFUL ESCAPE
you've been.

I remember looking you in the eyes, telling you that you're the only thing that truly mattered.

And you were, up until the point that you started telling me lies, messing with my mind. And the moment I started believing some of the things you were saying could be true is the moment I knew that I was LOSING ME, while LOVING YOU.

You always found pleasure in a fight, always needed to be right. But I finally realized, my self-love is the only thing that has ever truly mattered.

He drenched me
in gas,
lit the match
and tried
to convince me
I wasn't BURNING.

I have been the girl that couldn't
be tamed, since I was young.
That saying growing up as a child,
I still live by.
Except, I took out the young,
and now live WILD and FREE.

I've learned to be CAREFREE,
when it comes to something
as temporary as you.

The ground,
it shook with devotion.
But I was skating on THIN ICE.
I will end up PAYING a PRICE
for this love I cherish effortlessly.
But what is desire if not a gamble?
The ground beneath me is dark and cold,
yet I'll hold
you above the surface,
if this ice cracks.
I'll never let you be engulfed
by the frigid cold,
swallowed by DARKNESS.
I'll hold you alive,
and let my love keep you warm
til' you make it back to land.

I was finally FREE.
I walked the trail
straight from deceit,
leaving footprints in the snow,
as a reminder of which direction
to never go back to.

As the moonlight hits the frozen snow,
I see your GLITTERED LIES
sparkling like DIAMONDS,
all around me.

The most courage I will ever carry
is letting this love die,
rather than continuing to suffer in silence.

As the moonlight
hits the frozen snow,
I see your

glittered lies

sparkling like

diamonds

all around me.

I wish I was every SNOWFLAKE
that ever landed on your angelic face.
That I got to continuously taste you.
I wish I was every BLIZZARD
to ever surround you,
for the mere need to be engulfed in you.
I rage for you and your touch.
So if I must,
I will become every DROP of RAIN,
and every SNOWFLAKE
that ever gets the pleasure
to be upon you.

I live stuck inside my head,
a repeat of memories constantly
on attack.
Like the time you said "I'll be right back."
The door closed, never to open again.
So please just say "I LOVE YOU,"
never, "I'll see you soon."
Those words have been spoken and broken.
"I'll be right back"
are four words that leave my
soul cold, wondering if fate will allow us
to make it back to each other in time.

But "I LOVE YOU"
will be the words
I'll be okay to replay for all of time.

There was once a time
we were changing for the better,
in rainy weather,
watching the fog grow stronger.
We had every intention
to stay on the right path,
but it got cloudy fast.
Leaving us confused
on which way was right,
while doing all the wrong things
with each other.
We found ourselves with only us left,
laying in a BED of SIN.

You were CHAOS and CALM.
A timeless twilight.
You were the perfect mix
of LIFE and DEATH.
The perfect mix of
a HAUNTED HEART,
and a HOLY EMBRACE.
You were a hint of
HORRIFIC and HAPPY hues.
And though the paradox you were
became confusing,
I've never wanted to be lost
in something more than I did you.

Like snowflakes filling the air in a silent squall,
I find beauty within the storm that rages inside me.
All the madness left there from past sadness,
now swirling around in a beautiful vortex of white.
While I let go of the pain, I leave behind all the
shame, and my heartbreak disappears. Now I finally
find solace in the beauty that falls from the sky, long
awaited — this is my final GOODBYE.

As I bleed out these breaths, I need you to know your face, no matter my ending, will always be the last thing I picture. When these wrinkled lifelines are done growing old, I will picture you as sweet as an angel, smiling, and I will carry you with me wherever I shall go. But until then, I'll be right here dancing to the last song, before winter's frost. Knowing time goes fast, and the only thing I truly cherish is the warmth I'll feel from your body. As the cold sets in, these are the moments I want to be able to remember for ten thousand lifetimes. So as the nights grow darker, faster, however long we last here,
I will FALL FOR YOU
all over again, every morning.

I thought we had so much time,
but our love, it FLATLINED.
It stopped beating
and our star in the heavens
stopped shining.
It took me
LOVING and LOSING
you
to see
not all beautiful things
survive.

You had your head in the clouds,
and my mind was amongst the stars.
You were meant to chase the sun,
and I was meant to pursue the moon.
Dawn and dusk were our solitude.
The two times a day we came together.
We loved intensely, and perfectly
for a short time,
only to part in gratitude.
Knowing it's brief and
it'll soon return,
that's when I learned
to love ALL of YOU, briefly,
is better than loving only a
PIECE of YOU.

You looked at me like I belonged to the STARS.
Like I was something inexplicable to this world.
You looked at me with such an AWE.
I'll never again see it replicated.
That one look was a once in a lifetime moment.
It was a complete sonnet without syllables.
It was the moment I felt gravity leave,
and I felt everywhere all at once,
all because you looked at me in a way
that said "WELCOME HOME."

I have loved you for lifetimes and I have learned one
of two things,
first you may be my destiny.
In each life, no matter what life throws at us
we always will come back to each other.
Or maybe that the destruction I think you pull me out
from in my mind, is actually caused by you.
It hurts to love you, and love isn't supposed to hurt.
Yet I still can't escape you. I don't want too.
Nor will I ever try.
So while this storm of emotions awakens me
and carries me right back to the arms I miss,
I pray God sends the angels to reveal why we are
stuck in this spiritual push and pull.
I can't escape you.
My heart keeps coming home to you,
so what more can I do than love you
the way I feel God intends me to do.

I don't know where to go,
I can't find a place safe from
loving you anymore.
I watched a demon
walk into a church today,
and
since then,
I have realized there is no such thing
as a sanctuary.
Or that maybe you are my
only safe haven in this realm.
Your eyes didn't glow yellow,
in fact they were all my favorite hues.
And your smile made me forget
the words to my prayers.
You DISRUPT my life,
yet I am irrevocably intrigued with you.
I pray for FORGIVNESS,
for loving the bad boy who's making me
turn away from my religion,
and who's touch is sacrilegiously intoxicating.

I vow to love you despite all your dark ways.
Because if God created all things, he created you too.
And who am I to judge God's creation?
Maybe what's flawed to me is heavens need for
perfection. Because meeting you,
I've had to rethink all I've ever believed in.
I only know one single thing for sure,
I LOVE every one of your EBONY WAYS.

It's not punishment, it's preparation.

I keep repeating that in my head, but this is our final goodbye, and I can't lie… it feels more like punishment, every step further away from me you walk. I pray the angels come down, whisper in my ear, not to fear. Because I'm losing my faith as your image fades out. Full of doubt, I wonder what this can possibly be preparation for, except maybe the realization that to love you was beautiful, but to endure the pain of letting go is inevitable. And I can still love you now. I just have to learn how to get by with only memories.

Maybe life's preparation is only heartbreak.

Either way at least I got to LOVE YOU.

Im sorry. I'm sorry that I made you carry my burdens when they weren't yours to carry. I'm sorry that when life got tough for you I ran when you needed me to stay. I pray one day you'll see my spiral downward was mine alone, and I am sorry I grabbed your arm, and brought you down with me. I didn't foresee the pain I was causing, or how I was turning you into a mirror image of me, when you were perfect just the way you were. I wish I could turn back time and rewrite each wrong, but even with you loving me broken, you still turned out so strong. I applaud the person you fought to stay, and didn't break just because you felt we would be broken together. Thanks to you, I crawled out from despair, because you cared enough to share your strength. I'm sorry that you had to stay strong for the both of us. I hope you know it's you who taught me trust. I'm sorry I wasn't the person you deserved, when you needed me to be most.

I LOVED you without judgement.
I carried your faults like the sky carries the moon,
and did whatever I could to bring peace into your life.
But the stability I brought was overlooked and
unappreciated. You thought you needed more when
you already had it all. Now a bit cracked and bruised,
I'll walk away from everything I fought far too hard to
keep. Just remember, when I'm gone,
I don't owe you a god damn thing.

I'll condemn the sun,
strike down the moon,
and curse the earth
if it takes your hand
out from mine.
I'll destroy it all if it destroys us.
You're my reason for existing,
you're my earth,
my home.
So if this cruel world tries to take you,
we will go down together,
leaving no trace of this place
that has only ever been jealous of
the love we carry.
Jealous of something so strong.
It's imprinted into our soul,
like heavenly DNA.
So if they try,
I hope you know,
broken, bloody, and vengeful,
I'll only falter if I'm tasting your lips,
as we turn to dust.
Til' then, I will love you down
to the core of existence itself.
It's YOU and ME against the world.

I don't need a castle or a hero,
yet someone to see I'm a warrior,
myself.
Someone that will give
my heart a home to rest,
while my wounds turn to scars,
and we reach past the stars,
for a piece of heaven,
and the peace we both deserve,
here on earth together.

I stared at the FULL MOON and pictured you
next to me. I begged, pledged, and bargained on my
knees. If manifestation is real, have it bring you to me,
just once more. The longing I have in my soul for you
can be felt on moons in other worlds. So if this need
to survive is based upon my love for you, come home
to me, because until you do,
I'll be under every FULL MOON,
screaming "I love you" into the night's sky.

About the author:

Jessica Livia, also known as MLIVV, is poetry author, single mother, and widow, who believes in expressing herself through the magic of words. She writes to share with the world her belief that there is a such thing as love after death, for love never truly dies.

To keep up with the author, follow her social media handles:

Instagram: @mlivvpoet
Tiktok: @mlivvpoet

Acknowledgements

To my M's:

Matthew & Matina, I've had the honor to love you both. That's enough inspiration for a thousand lifetimes. I love you two more than words can convey. Matthew, my love, be with us always.

Melissa Combs, without you, I couldn't have done this. Thanks to meeting you, I have a best friend, a beautiful publisher, and a bright soul to guide me. Thank you and I love you for all you do.

Mommy, you are my best friend, and my idol. I hope to be even half the mother you are. I love you so much.

Octave Eight

PUBLISHING

∞

Instagram: @octaveeightpublishing

Tiktok: @octaveeightpoetry

Email: octaveeightpublishing@gmail.com

Made in the USA
Middletown, DE
18 November 2023

43018192R00126